AF228147

Edmund Kemper

The Co-Ed Killer

by Judy Dodge Cummings

Essential Library

An Imprint of Abdo Publishing
abdobooks.com

ABDOBOOKS.COM

Published by Abdo Publishing, a division of ABDO, PO Box 398166, Minneapolis, Minnesota 55439. Copyright © 2025 by Abdo Consulting Group, Inc. International copyrights reserved in all countries. No part of this book may be reproduced in any form without written permission from the publisher. Essential Library™ is a trademark and logo of Abdo Publishing.

Printed in China.
102024
012025

Cover Photo: Album/Alamy
Interior Photos: Morgan Ong/AP Images, 4–5; Seth Poppel/Yearbook Library, 6; Jerry Telfer/San Francisco Chronicle/Hearst Newspapers/Getty Images, 8, 78–79, 84; Shutterstock Images, 12–13, 14, 17, 50, 64, 70; Africa Studio/Shutterstock Images, 19; Canyon Light Photography/Alamy, 22–23; David Cole/Alamy, 26; Atascadero State Hospital Photographic Records, 27; Peggy Peattie/ZUMA Press, Inc./Alamy, 30; Bettmann/Getty Images, 34–35, 67, 68–69, 88–89, 90, 93; Chris Howes/Wild Places Photography/Alamy, 37; Ted Streshinsky/Corbis Historical/Getty Images, 40; Western Mail Archive/Mirrorpix/Getty Images, 43; Bettmann Archive/Getty Images, 44–45, 81; Yevhenii Slivin/Shutterstock Images, 47; John Carl D'Annibale/Albany Times Union/Hearst Newspapers/Getty Images, 53; Carolyn Van Houten/The Washington Post/Getty Images, 55; Robert Natkin/Archive Photos/Getty Images, 56–57; lucky-photographer/Alamy, 60; Heritage Art/Heritage Images/Hulton Archive/Getty Images, 63; Harold M. Lambert/Archive Photos/Getty Images, 77; Lea Suzuki/San Francisco Chronicle/Hearst Newspapers/Getty Images, 97; Dmitriy Shironosov/Alamy, 98

Editor: Marley Richmond
Series Designer: Joshua Olson

Library of Congress Control Number: 2024938303

PUBLISHER'S CATALOGING-IN-PUBLICATION DATA

Names: Cummings, Judy Dodge, author.
Title: Edmund Kemper: the co-ed killer / by Judy Dodge Cummings
Other title: the co-ed killer
Description: Minneapolis, Minnesota: ABDO Publishing, 2025 | Series: Serial killers | Includes online resources and index.
Identifiers: ISBN 9781098295332 (lib. bdg.) | ISBN 9798384916338 (eBook)
Subjects: LCSH: Kemper, Edmund, 1948- --Juvenile literature. | Co-ed Killer, 1948- --Juvenile literature. | Killers (Murderers)--Biographies--Juvenile literature. | Serial killers--Biographies--Juvenile literature. | Crime--Juvenile literature. | True crime stories--Juvenile literature.
Classification: DDC 364.15232--dc23

CONTENTS

This book discusses accounts of crime, violence, and death that may be disturbing to some readers.

GONE MISSING

On the evening of September 14, 1972, Aiko Koo waited at a bus stop in Berkeley, California. The slender, dark-haired 15-year-old was headed to a dance studio in San Francisco. A dancer since age four, Aiko was making a name for herself in traditional Korean ballet. She had performed for a United Nations celebration at age 12 and was now winning college dance scholarships. She had recently been selected to perform at an upcoming festival in Saint Louis, Missouri.

While she waited for the bus, Aiko struck up a conversation with another girl at the bus stop. They chatted about school and their families. After a few minutes, Aiko told the girl that she was tired of waiting for the bus. It was important for her to get to class on time, and there was a faster way to get there: hitchhiking.

Just that afternoon, Aiko's mother had warned her not to catch a ride with a stranger. She said it was dangerous.

The 1940s through the 1960s were known as the golden era of hitchhiking. In the decades that followed, people started to see hitchhiking as a dangerous way to travel.

Still, Aiko had hitched before. Lots of girls did it without anything bad happening.

So Aiko scribbled her desired destination on a piece of paper and held it toward oncoming traffic. Minutes later, a light-colored car pulled up. The tall, brown-haired man behind the wheel watched as Aiko hesitated a moment and then climbed into the passenger seat.

Missing Person

Aiko's mother was Skaidrite Rubene Koo, a Lithuanian immigrant and single parent. Koo did not own a car.

Aiko Koo was a high schooler when she disappeared.

Normally, Aiko attended dance class locally, but she had received a special invitation to an advanced class in San Francisco. Koo typically accompanied her daughter to class. However, that evening she was busy putting the finishing touches on the traditional costume Aiko would wear for the festival. So Koo let her daughter go alone with a warning: Do not hitchhike!

Koo worked hard to secure Aiko's future. She paid for her to attend specialized Korean ballet classes. Sewing Aiko's dance costumes was time consuming too. Photographs of the girl's performances show her dressed in long flowing gowns with elaborate headdresses.

As Koo worked, the hours ticked by. The time that Aiko should have been home came and went. Koo called the dance studio and learned that Aiko never arrived at class. At about midnight, she called the police and reported her daughter missing. Koo expected the police to act quickly. Instead, an officer told her to relax. Aiko was probably just breaking curfew.

Koo could not relax. She called the police repeatedly until the next day, when they finally sent an officer to her house. "She's been kidnapped!" Koo told the officer. "I've had a premonition all summer that something was going to happen to change our lives."[1] The officer tried to comfort Koo. Maybe Aiko had run away. If so, she would come home soon. He urged Koo not to despair. So she kept waiting.

Kemper's vehicle did not look suspicious from the outside.

Record Expunged

A few days after Aiko went missing, a dirty, bug-splattered yellow Ford sedan pulled up in front of a psychiatrists' office in Fresno, California, almost 200 miles (320 km) from where Aiko had gone missing. A giant of a man emerged from the car. Six feet, nine inches (2.06 m) tall and 280 pounds (127 kg), 23-year-old Edmund Kemper was there to meet two court-appointed psychiatrists. This appointment would make or break his future.

Kemper wore gold-rimmed glasses and kept his brown hair and mustache trimmed short and neat. He unlocked the trunk of his car, peeked inside, and sniffed.

Then he slammed the lid, locked the trunk, and entered the building.

Kemper met with the psychiatrists for several hours. He needed both doctors to tell the court that he was no longer a threat to society. If they did, the Madera County Superior Court judge would seal Kemper's juvenile police record. This legal process strictly limits who can have access to information about crimes someone committed before the age of 18.

It is hard to find a good job if a potential employer knows that the applicant has been convicted of double homicide, and that was the case for Kemper. When he was 15, Kemper murdered his grandparents. Medical experts found that he was legally insane at the time. Therefore, instead of serving time in a juvenile detention facility, Kemper spent five years in the Atascadero State Hospital for the Criminally Insane.[2]

INSANITY PLEA

The term *insanity* has not been used as a diagnosis by medical professionals for a century. *Insanity* is a legal term, not a medical one. The legal definition of insanity is when a criminal has a mental illness that makes it impossible for them to know they are committing a crime or to understand that their actions are wrong. This does not make the person innocent, but it can affect the type and length of punishment they receive.

Kemper did well in the institution. He followed the rules, completed his General Educational Development (GED) program, and responded to therapy. The staff at Atascadero viewed Kemper as a success story. He was released from state custody in 1969, determined to begin life over. The young man dreamed of a career as a police officer. To get such a job, Kemper needed his past to remain secret.

Later that September day, Kemper emerged from the psychiatrists' office full of confidence. The meetings had gone well. The face Kemper showed these doctors was that of an intelligent, well-adjusted young man, ready to fully rejoin society. On November 29, 1972, Kemper's juvenile record was sealed. Now he would not have to reveal his convictions to others.

As Kemper approached his car, he considered opening the trunk again. Then he noticed a fly buzzing around the bumper and changed his mind. He left the trunk closed and drove away.

Still Waiting

Meanwhile, Skaidrite Rubene Koo did not believe her daughter was a runaway. She plastered posters of Aiko all over Berkeley and alerted the newspapers to her daughter's disappearance. Koo and her friends and family waited at bus stations, night after night. They showed strangers a photo of Aiko and asked if they had seen the girl. Koo wrote to police departments in California, Oregon, and Washington, and she even contacted the Federal Bureau of Investigation (FBI). All leads were dead ends.

Koo pinned Aiko's traditional ballet dress to the wall in her home. On the floor beneath it sat the ceremonial drums Aiko used in her performances. They would remain there for months, waiting for Aiko's return.

Koo would never see her daughter again. Kemper was the last person to see Aiko alive. When Kemper left the psychiatrists' office, Aiko Koo's severed head was in the trunk of his car.

> **"I would see no psychiatric reason to consider him to be of any danger to himself or to any member of society."[3]**
>
> *–A psychiatrist who recommended Kemper's juvenile record be sealed*

CHAPTER 2

A TROUBLED CHILDHOOD

Edmund Kemper's childhood planted the seeds for the troubled man he became. He was born on December 18, 1948, in Burbank, California. His parents, Edmund II and Clarnell Kemper, nicknamed their only son "Guy." He had two sisters. Susan was six years older, and Allyn was two years younger.

The Kemper household teemed with conflict. Edmund II had been in combat during World War II (1939–1945). He returned home from Europe with medals, weapons, and war stories. Edmund's parents argued about finances and their children. Of his wife, Edmund II said, "Suicide missions in wartime . . . were nothing compared to living with her."[1]

Clarnell thought her anger was justified. She believed her husband was too stern with his daughters and pampered his son. "All he ever gave Ed was his medals and war stories," Clarnell said.[2] But Edmund liked his father's

Children who frequently see their parents argue may have an increased chance of being anxious, angry, or violent when they grow up.

tales of war and was fascinated by the knives, guns, and bayonets Edmund II left around the house.

In 1957, Edmund's parents separated. Clarnell moved the children to Helena, Montana, and took a job at a local bank. She began drinking heavily. Edmund felt abandoned by his father, and his relationship with his mother deteriorated.

When Edmund was eight years old, his mother made him sleep in the basement. Each night, she moved the kitchen table and lifted the trapdoor beneath it, and

Edmund descended creaky steps into the dark, dank space. An old furnace sat in one corner. Two bare bulbs dangling from the ceiling provided dim light. When Edmund cried that he did not want to sleep in the basement, Clarnell smacked him in the head.

Edmund did not understand why he had to sleep in this dungeon while his sisters and mother slept upstairs. He spent long winter nights staring at the grate in the furnace. He described it as "staring into the fires of hell" and made bargains with the devil to spare his life.[3]

In 1958, Edmund II moved back in with his family. He was horrified that Edmund was forced to sleep in the

Edmund was terrified of sleeping in the basement.

basement, and he confronted his wife. Clarnell claimed she worried the boy would molest one of his sisters. Her daughters had told her that Edmund said he wanted to kiss his teacher but could only do so if he killed her first. Edmund II still demanded his son be allowed to return to his bedroom. If not, he would report Clarnell to the police.

Although Edmund's father had come to his son's rescue, he did not hang around. Edmund II returned to California. The couple officially divorced in 1961. Two months later, Edmund II remarried to a woman with a son two years older than Edmund. Edmund's father had abandoned him once again.

A FAN OF JOHN WAYNE

When Edmund was young, television heroes became substitutes for his absent father. Edmund II had a loud voice, large body, and small feet, and Edmund thought his dad resembled movie star John Wayne. On a trip to Hollywood, Edmund visited Grauman's Chinese Theater, where John Wayne's footprints were cast in concrete on the sidewalk. Edmund stepped onto Wayne's prints. Later he said, "I was proud to see that my feet were bigger than his."[4]

Violent Tendencies Emerge

From a young age, Edmund's personality was a strange mix of daring and danger. During a trip to New York City, the family went to the top of the Empire State Building.

Without warning, Edmund dashed toward the edge. His aunt hauled him back.

Seemingly thrilled by risk, Edmund often shocked his friends by lying spread-eagle in the street. Cars screeched to a halt. Drivers leaped out, terrified they had struck someone. Edmund would jump up, laugh, and run away. He did not explain why he acted this way.

The relationship among the three Kemper siblings was also full of tension. After his sister Allyn broke Edmund's cap gun, he snapped off the head of her Barbie doll. This revenge was not enough, so he sliced off the doll's hands as well.

Edmund seemed to need to punish himself. He invented a game called Gas Chamber. He ordered the girls to tie him up in the living room recliner. Then Edmund would stiffen, tremble violently, and pretend to die.

FIRST BEHEADING

At age eight, Edmund watched a magic show where a fake guillotine sat center stage. This machine would normally be used to behead a person. The magician put a potato in the apparatus and asked for a volunteer. A 16-year-old girl stepped up and put her head in the brace. When the magician dropped the blade, the audience gasped. But only the potato was sliced in half while the girl walked away unharmed. The sight was seared into Edmund's mind. Of this incident, he later said, "The concept of it was so raw, and it was titillating."[5] Later in life, he developed a disturbing fascination with beheadings.

Showing cruelty to animals, such as killing and burying a family pet, may be a sign that a child is struggling at home or does not know how to communicate their feelings.

Eventually pretend death was not enough. When Edmund was ten years old, he buried the family cat alive. The boy later dug up the suffocated cat and cut off its head.

On a summer afternoon three years later, Edmund was alone in his bedroom sharpening his knife and his father's machete. The boy's Siamese cat slept in a chair beside him. Recently, the cat had seemed more affectionate to Edmund's sisters than to him. This fact suddenly enraged the boy. He seized the cat by its nape and stabbed the animal until it died. Terrified of being discovered, Edmund buried the cat in the yard. However, he kept some of the animal's body parts, hiding them in his closet.

The Struggle to Fit In

Edmund did not fit in at home or in the community. "I always felt like a social outcast," he recalled in an interview years later. "I never managed to find my place."[6]

–Edmund Kemper, describing how his thought patterns changed after puberty

At age 13, Edmund shot the dog of a neighborhood boy. From then on, no other boys would befriend him. Edmund was teased, intimidated, and chased through the neighborhood.

Edmund did no better with girls. As a young teen, Edmund was approached by a pretty classmate. She flirted with him. Although Edmund was attracted to her, he backed away. "It terrified me," he later recalled, "because I didn't know how to react or control the emotions that germinated in me."[7]

Although Edmund was very intelligent, he did not find refuge in books or learning. He was disobedient in class. The boy daydreamed constantly. His fantasies were rooted in violence. He talked to a school counselor a couple of times, but the counselor did not delve into Edmund's emotional well-being. Edmund was left to wrestle alone with his troubled mind.

Nowhere to Call Home

Arguments between Edmund and his mother were fierce and frequent. He believed she favored his sisters, and he hated her nagging. Clarnell, a large woman who stood six feet (1.83 m) tall, forced Edmund's obedience by whipping him with a belt, buckle side down. She ordered her son not to scream, telling him this "so the neighbors don't think I'm beating you."[9]

Research studies show that approximately one-third of convicted serial killers have experienced physical abuse, such as being beaten with a belt.

Edmund felt like a ping-pong ball as he bounced from one relative's house to another. Whenever he would run away from his mother's house to join his dad, Edmund II quickly shipped the boy back. But after Edmund spent a short time living with Clarnell, she would send him to live with his grandparents. It seemed no one wanted him.

On Thanksgiving Day in 1963, 14-year-old Edmund hopped on a bus to Los Angeles, California, where his father now lived with his new family. The teen complained about how horrible life was with his mother. Edmund II agreed to let his son live with him, but only temporarily. Edmund was thrilled. However, he did not tell his father that the real reason he had run away was because he was plagued by fantasies of killing his mother.

Edmund's vision of a happy home would not come true. At Christmas a few weeks later, his father took

Edmund to visit his paternal grandparents in North Fork, California. When Christmas dinner ended, Edmund II drove away alone. His new wife did not want her stepson living with them. To add salt to the wound, Edmund II got an unlisted phone number. Edmund could no longer contact his father. This was yet another abandonment for Edmund.

Clarnell called her ex-husband and warned him about the risk he was taking by leaving their son with his grandparents. "[Edmund] is a really funny bird," she told her ex. "You may be surprised to wake up one morning to learn that [the grandparents] have been killed."[10]

CHAPTER 3

MURDER AND ATASCADERO

The small town of North Fork, California, sits in the foothills of the Sierra Nevada mountain range. To 15-year-old Edmund, his grandparents' ranch there seemed like the end of the earth. He hated living there.

Grandpa Edmund Kemper I was 72 years old and a retired employee of the California Division of Highways. Grandma Maude, 66, wrote children's stories. Edmund called his grandfather "senile" and said his grandmother "was constantly emasculating me and my grandfather."[1]

Kemper felt isolated while living in rural North Fork, California.

Edmund enrolled in the Sierra Joint Union High School in the town of Tollhouse. Unlike his previous school experience, Edmund followed the rules and maintained his grades. His grandparents thought the teen had adjusted well when the school year ended in 1964, so Edmund was allowed to visit his mother and sisters in Montana. But when the boy returned to his grandparents' ranch in August, he was grumpy and depressed.

Tensions Build

One pastime Edmund enjoyed was shooting the .22 rifle his grandfather had given him for Christmas. Grandma Maude didn't like when her grandson killed animals, but Edmund I paid the boy a bounty for every rabbit and gopher he shot. Edmund I did order his grandson not to shoot any birds. Edmund ignored the order. As punishment, Edmund's grandparents took the gun away from him for a while. Edmund blamed his grandmother for this, and he resented her.

Worried about the influence of other teenagers, his grandmother gave Edmund strict rules. He was not allowed to hang out with kids in town or bring them home. Cartoons were banned. Grandma cautioned Edmund that if he did not learn to follow rules, he would not be allowed to live with his father again. "I couldn't please her," Edmund recalled. "It was like being in jail. . . . I was a walking time bomb."[3]

The Bomb Explodes

On August 27, 1964, Edmund I was in town doing errands, and Maude was typing at the kitchen table. She noticed Edmund staring at her with a zombielike expression. She told him to stop looking at her like that.

Edmund grabbed his rifle off the rack and told his grandma that he was going rabbit hunting. "Oh, you'd better not be shooting those birds again," Maude said.[4] Those would be her last words.

Edmund stepped out onto the front porch. The rage that had been simmering inside him for days boiled over. He turned around, raised the gun, and fired through the screen. He shot Maude twice in the head and once in the back. Then Edmund grabbed a knife from the kitchen and stabbed his grandmother several times in the back.

The .22 rifle is a popular gun for hunting small animals such as rabbits and birds. However, these guns are still powerful enough to hurt or kill a human.

After wrapping her head in a towel, Edmund dragged her body to the bedroom.

A few minutes later, Edmund I returned. Edmund watched as his grandfather parked by the garage and began to unload bags. While the elderly man's back was turned, Edmund snuck up behind him and shot him in the back of the head. Then the boy dragged his grandfather into the garage. Edmund washed his hands and tried to wash away the blood pooling in the dirt beside the truck. He pulled his grandfather's body into the house and stuffed it in a closet.

Now Edmund's mind began to reel. He had just killed two people. What should his next step be? Edmund's first instinct was to kill anyone who came by. "If I had been in a [crowded] city," Edmund said later, "I would have been a mass murderer at 15."[5]

Soon the boy's rage dwindled, and fear set in. He called his mother. "Grandma is dead and so is Grandpa," he said.[6] Clarnell told Edmund to wait while she called the local sheriff. Edmund himself also called the police.

When the police arrived, Edmund was waiting on the porch. He confessed to the murders almost immediately. When the police asked why he had killed his grandparents, Edmund said, "I just wanted to see what it felt like to kill Grandma."[7] Edmund I was a different story. Edmund did not want him to suffer when he discovered his wife was dead, so Edmund shot him too. Now Edmund knew what it felt like to kill someone. It was a feeling he would not forget.

Edmund had a mugshot taken when he was arrested for murdering his grandparents.

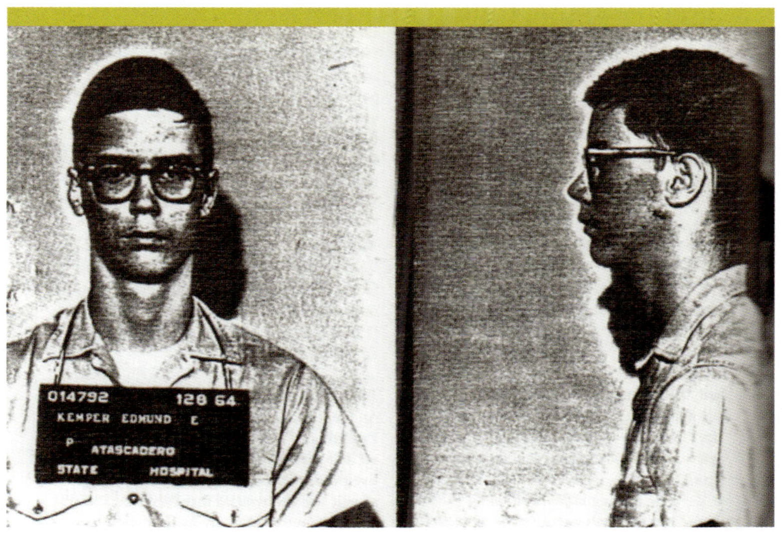

Judged Insane

After Edmund was arrested, a court-appointed psychiatrist diagnosed him with paranoid schizophrenia. Schizophrenia is a mental illness. One of its symptoms is psychosis, which is when a person loses touch with reality. A person experiencing an episode of psychosis may see, hear, and believe things that are not real. Paranoia is a form of disordered thinking in which a person is unreasonably suspicious of other people, believing that others are trying to harm or manipulate them. The psychiatrist declared that Edmund was a danger to himself and others.

This diagnosis benefited his case by helping explain his actions. He was declared legally insane, which meant the teen had not understood what he was doing when he murdered his grandparents and could not control himself. Therefore, instead of being locked up in a juvenile detention center or a prison, Edmund would receive treatment in a psychiatric hospital.

Edmund was sent to the Atascadero State Hospital for the Criminally Insane. Edmund entered this secure institution on December 6, 1964. He would spend the rest of his childhood there.

Refuge at Atascadero

Atascadero State Hospital opened its doors in 1954. The all-male hospital was located on the central coast of California, halfway between San Francisco and Los Angeles. Patients did not voluntarily spend time at Atascadero. County courts or the Department of Corrections sent them.

When Edmund was admitted to Atascadero, roughly 1,600 inmates lived there. Hallways, wards, and the cafeteria overflowed with too many men for the size of the institution. Among them were a few dozen murderers and more than 800 sex offenders.[9] Edmund, who was then 15, was far younger than most other inmates. Despite being surrounded by men twice his age, Atascadero was a refuge for the boy. "Basically, I was born there," Edmund recalled. "I have a lot of fond memories of the place."[10]

For the first time in his life, Edmund believed he was treated as a person struggling with an illness instead of being told what a bad person he was. Staff put him

Atascadero State Hospital remains open as a secure facility for criminals who need mental health treatment.

through a series of tests and eventually rejected the earlier diagnosis of paranoid schizophrenia. Edmund did not see or hear things that were not real. Instead, he sulked, argued, and complained of being misunderstood. Throughout his sentence, doctors diagnosed him with a series of other mental illnesses, including borderline, dependent, antisocial, and avoidant personality disorders.

IQ tests revealed that Edmund scored in the top percentile. According to those tests, he was smarter than 99 percent of the population. William Schanberger, a doctor who saw the teen regularly, remarked, "Ed is a bright fellow. That was obvious when you talked to him."[11]

Edmund seemed to thrive at Atascadero and was a model patient. The Junior Chamber of Commerce (Jaycees) invited him to join. This global organization believes in religious faith, economic justice, global cooperation, and the value of service work. The Jaycees gave Edmund a membership pin, which he wore proudly for years.

Edmund seemed eager to recover his mental health. He willingly took psychological tests, attended individual and group therapy, and gave interviews to anyone who asked. Edmund responded so well to treatment that the hospital's chief psychologist eventually made him crew leader of the psychological testing lab.

In this role, Edmund administered tests to other patients and helped develop a new psychological test. The director of research at the time, psychologist Frank Vanasek, saw the pride Kemper took in his work as a sign of the boy's recovery. "A sociopath would have been more likely to use his performance to achieve other ends," the doctor said.[12]

Con Job

Little did the doctor know, this was exactly what Edmund was doing. He wanted out of Atascadero, and he would lie to get himself released. While he took the psychological tests, Edmund learned what the doctors wanted to hear and strategically fed them these answers.

Edmund was succeeding. It was hard work, Edmund recalled. "I was the dynamic young man, and [the doctors] began to say maybe we can let him out sooner than we had thought."[13]

Despite his ulterior motives, Edmund's time in Atascadero gave him new insights. "I found out," he later said, "that I really killed my grandmother because I wanted to kill my mother."[14] Edmund began to recognize how destructive his relationship with his mother was.

Edmund also learned other, more dangerous lessons at Atascadero. He socialized with inmates convicted of rape and murder. These men were happy to share the details of their crimes with this youth who listened eagerly. He noted their techniques and their mistakes. Meanwhile, Edmund's violent fantasies grew stronger. During his years at Atascadero, his desires morphed into dreams of sex and murder combined.

Edmund never revealed these fantasies to his therapists. Confessing such dark thoughts would have kept him locked up forever, he thought. Edmund was too

–Edmund Kemper, discussing a fantasy he had as a teen

smart for that. "I hid it from them. [The doctors] can't see
the things going on in my mind. All I had to do to conceal
it from them was not talk
about it."[16]

Released

Edmund's con worked.
Doctors at Atascadero
became convinced he was
cured of mental illnesses. On
December 18, 1969, Edmund
walked out of Atascadero as a
free man.

Edmund's doctors thought
he was ready to return to
society. But they weren't aware
of the secrets Edmund had kept.
In addition, US culture had transformed dramatically in
his years behind bars. Edmund would not adapt well to
these changes.

THE MANSON MURDERS

Just a few months before Kemper was released from Atascadero, another California murderer dominated the headlines. On August 9, 1969, members of a cult led by Charles Manson killed five people in the home of a famous movie director.[17] Two days later, they murdered a supermarket executive and his wife. Although Manson did not kill anyone himself, he was convicted of masterminding the plot. Later, Kemper and Manson were housed in the same prison ward. Manson died behind bars in 2017.

CHAPTER 4

BACK ON THE STREETS

The 1960s drew to a close days after 21-year-old Kemper was released. Much had changed while he was gone. Humans had landed on the moon. Civil rights movements expanded equality for people of color and women. The Vietnam War (1954–1975) raged. Hippies, members of a counterculture movement, preached love and peace.

In this new world, Kemper felt ill at ease. "When I got out on the street," he told a journalist, "it was like being on a strange planet."[1] Young people spoke and thought differently than they had before Kemper was locked up. Kemper began to struggle mentally and emotionally.

Living with Mom

Doctors at Atascadero had repeatedly advised Kemper not to move back in with his mother. This living arrangement distressed him. Yet that is exactly what he did.

The anti-war social movement grew while Kemper was behind bars. Protests and marches were common in California during the late 1960s and early 1970s.

While Kemper was hospitalized, his mother had married and divorced for a third time. Now she lived in Santa Cruz, California, where she worked as an administrative assistant on the college campus there.

After Kemper moved into his mother's duplex, the fighting began immediately. Clarnell remained a heavy drinker. She showed no problems during the day at her job, but in the evening, she frequently attacked Kemper. She said he lacked ambition. She accused him of drinking too much and not working hard enough. Clarnell also blamed Kemper for her failed relationships. She said, "No one wants to be with me out of fear of you."[2]

Dreams Crushed

Kemper worked a series of laborer jobs until he was hired by the California Division of Highways in 1971. His colleagues nicknamed him Forklift because he could carry a 92-pound (42 kg) bag of cement under each arm. The steady paycheck allowed Kemper to move into an apartment with a friend. However, unable to manage money or the friendship, Kemper often wound up back at his mother's house.

The job with the highway department bored Kemper.

"My mother and I started right in on horrendous battles ... and just over stupid things. I remember one roof-raiser was over whether I should have my teeth cleaned."[3]

–Edmund Kemper, describing his relationship with Clarnell

He dreamed of becoming a California Highway Patrolman. Cruising the highways on a motorcycle with a gun and the authority that came with a uniform appealed to Kemper. He enrolled in criminal law classes at a local community college, but then he discovered law enforcement positions had a maximum height limit. Kemper was too tall to become a police officer.

It is illegal for anyone who is not a police officer to own a real police badge and use it to impersonate a police officer.

In consolation, Kemper bought himself a motorcycle so he could at least look the part. He often went to a bar near the county courthouse called the Jury Room. The place was a favorite hangout for off-duty cops. Kemper befriended some officers, and one man gave him a training police badge and a pair of handcuffs.

In February 1971, an automobile struck Kemper while he was driving his motorcycle. He severely injured one arm. Kemper sued the driver and won a settlement worth roughly $100,000 in 2024 dollars.[4] Because he had to wear a cast for months, Kemper received medical leave from work. Now he had plenty of time and money.

Trying to Connect

A few months after his release from custody, Kemper went on his first date. It was a disaster. At the time in life when many teenagers learned how to flirt and have their first kiss, Kemper had been locked up. He felt socially awkward.

This sense of failure increased the darkness seeping into Kemper's mind. With some of the insurance settlement money, he bought a yellow two-door Ford Galaxie 500. Kemper equipped the car to resemble a police cruiser with a radio transmitter, microphone, and whip antenna. In his free time, he cruised the streets and highways.

Picking Up Co-Eds

The coastal communities of California are beautiful, with miles of beaches, mountains, streams, and redwood forests. The region is home to several colleges and universities. The University of California, Santa Cruz, sits on a thickly wooded campus encompassing 2,000 acres (810 ha).[6] About 30 miles (48 km) northeast is the campus of San Jose State University. A little farther north is the University of California, Berkeley.

With college campuses came co-eds. Co-ed is a slang term that was primarily used in the 1970s for a female student attending a co-educational school, where men and women study together. Many students lived off campus, and most did not own cars. So they hitchhiked, a common method of getting from place to place in the 1970s.

In his new car, Kemper cruised 300 miles (480 km) north to the Oregon border and as far south as Santa Barbara.[7] Along the way, he picked up hitchhikers, mostly college-aged women. At first, he just wanted to chat and make friends with people his own age.

Kemper studied the women he picked up, trying to determine what made them uneasy and what

The University of California, Berkeley, was built as a co-educational facility. Men and women studied together at the university and at others across California.

relaxed them. When he realized his close-cropped hair made them suspicious, he grew it out, adding sideburns and a mustache, which was a look most young men wore back then.

But the change in appearance did not get Kemper far. He was tongue-tied and awkward. "I found myself doing things in an attempt to make things fit together inside. . . . It wasn't working."[9] When Kemper dropped the co-ed hitchhikers off, he usually felt frustrated and disrespected.

Kemper fantasized about women falling in love with him. But these daydreams clashed with his awareness of his own social awkwardness. So, he altered the fantasies.

If women would not fall in love with him, then Kemper would rape them. However, he recalled the convicted rapists at Atascadero who had all been caught. Rapists left witnesses, and witnesses talked. So, Kemper's fantasies morphed again, this time including murder. "I decided to mix the two," Kemper later admitted, "and have a situation of rape and murder and no witnesses and no prosecution."[10]

Practice Runs

Kemper outfitted his car with what he called a kill kit. Knives, towels, ropes, handcuffs, belts, and heavy-duty garbage bags went into the trunk. He draped a blue velveteen blanket over the back seat.

For more than a year, Kemper dropped off hitchhikers unharmed. He estimated he gave at least 150 women rides.[11] Eventually Kemper upped the ante. He took diversions rather than a direct route to the hitchhiker's destination. He gauged the women's unease when he did this and assessed his own physical and emotional response to their fear. Each time he picked up a rider, he came a little closer to the act he was preparing to perform.

Years later, Kemper explained how he teased himself by being a bit bolder with each hitchhiker he picked up. "It's a daring kind of thing. First, there wasn't a gun. . . . And then a gun is in the car. . . . It was like drugs. It was like alcohol. A little isn't enough."[12]

Kemper waited for the perfect moment to kill the perfect hitchhiker. He wanted to be far away from Santa Cruz so as not to cast any suspicion on himself. Now it was just a question of where, when, and who.

Kemper was not the only person who saw picking up hitchhikers as an opportunity to find victims to murder.

CHAPTER 5

THE CO-ED KILLER STRIKES

On May 7, 1972, Kemper dressed in what would become his usual murder clothing. He wore a light brown checkered shirt, a fringed buckskin jacket, and jeans dark enough to hide blood. Then he drove north to the University of California, Berkeley.

Kemper drove slowly, watching the college women as they headed to class. On Ashby Avenue, he spotted his targets. It was not one woman, but two. They were young, of average height, and pretty. One woman held a sign that said Stanford, indicating that they needed a ride to a college campus to the south.

Kemper said he often picked up hitchhikers who he thought were physically attractive.

CRETARY
OF POLICE

Kemper rolled down the window and told the women he was headed that way. They climbed in. From a few questions, Kemper determined neither woman was familiar with the area. He knew the area well from working for the highway department.

The First Time

The co-eds were Mary Anne Pesce and Anita Luchessa. They were 18-year-old roommates attending Fresno State College a few hours away. They had come to the area to visit friends at Berkeley and Stanford.

When Kemper turned down a rural road, he caught Pesce staring at him in the rearview mirror. For months he had picked up hitchhikers without harming them. "I was scared," he said later. "But I was determined."[1] This time would be different.

Kemper had stashed a borrowed handgun under his seat. Now he pulled it out and threatened the young women. They asked what he wanted. "You know what I want," Kemper said, implying he was going to rape them.[2] He pulled off on a deserted road.

Kemper handcuffed Pesce to the seat belt hook in the back seat and ordered Luchessa to get into the trunk. "Please don't do this," she cried.[3] Kemper forced her into

Kemper tried to suffocate Pesce with the belt from a bathrobe.

the trunk and returned to Pesce. His plan was to suffocate her—a bloodless, quiet death.

Kemper put a plastic bag over Pesce's head and tried to strangle her with a cloth belt. But the belt snapped, and Pesce bit a hole in the bag. Enraged, Kemper stabbed her in the back, side, and stomach multiple times. Pesce tried to call her friend's name.

Murder was messier and more time-consuming than Kemper had expected. He wanted to end it. He slashed Pesce's throat, and she lost consciousness immediately.

Kemper was shaken but had no time to regroup. "I knew I had to do it to the other girl right then," he recalled. "Because she had heard all the struggle, and she must have known something very serious was going on."[4]

Kemper went to the back of the car and raised the trunk lid, trying to conceal his bloody hands. But Luchessa saw the blood, and her lips began to tremble. To calm Luchessa, Kemper said Pesce had gotten smart with him. He might have broken her nose. He said Pesce needed Luchessa's help.

As the young woman began to climb out of the trunk, Kemper stabbed her. But she was wearing thick coveralls, and the blade did not even pierce the fabric. "Oh God! Oh God!" Luchessa cried and threw herself back into the trunk.[5]

Luchessa kicked and punched as Kemper tried to slash her throat. He wound up cutting his own hand. Kemper thrust the knife into her chest multiple times. The blade went in deep, but Luchessa kept struggling.

She screamed, a piercing cry that echoed through the woods. Kemper heard voices in the distance and knew he had to act fast. He jabbed at Luchessa's eyes but wound up only knocking off her glasses. However, the multiple wounds were taking their toll. Luchessa's cries became moans, and her limbs moved more slowly. Kemper stood back and watched.

When she stopped moving, Kemper threw his knife in the trunk and slammed the lid. He shoved Pesce's body onto the floor of the back seat and covered her with a jacket. Kemper drove out of the area, sweating profusely and with hands covered in blood. He passed two couples who seemed to be house hunting. Kemper forced a relaxed expression on his face as he drove by. They paid him no attention.

The Aftermath

At this time, Kemper was living alone in an apartment in Alameda. As he headed home, red and blue lights flashed in his rearview mirror. Kemper pulled to the side of the road and gripped the knife hidden under his leg.

The police officer who pulled him over informed Kemper that one of his taillights was busted. Luchessa had probably kicked it out while trapped in the trunk. Kemper transformed. Gone was the man who had just butchered two women. In his place was a pleasant, chatty person. Kemper thanked the officer and promised to fix the light.

Someone in a car's trunk could try to kick through the taillight to signal for help. Taillights may be broken in car accidents, so a broken taillight does not always look suspicious.

The cop did not notice the slash on Kemper's hand, the blood on his clothes, or the corpse in the back seat of his car.

Back at his apartment, Kemper undressed the bodies. He dismembered them, limb by limb, and decapitated them. Then Kemper performed sexual acts with the bodies, a practice called necrophilia. Finally, Kemper packed the body parts into garbage bags. Throughout the process, Kemper snapped Polaroid photographs to preserve the memory.

Once his adrenaline rush ended, Kemper reflected on what he had done. "I was suicidal, very disturbed," he said.[6] Kemper recognized how he had manipulated the young women into trusting him, and now he felt guilty.

The next morning, Kemper loaded the bagged body parts into his trunk. He headed to Loma Prieta, the highest peak in the Santa Cruz Mountains. He tossed Pesce's corpse in a grove of trees along a mountain road and dumped Luchessa's in a thicket near a small hill.

Kemper made a mental map of the trees, rocks, and bushes near the body parts so he could find his way back in the future. As for the women's heads, Kemper kept them until they became too rotten. Then he hurled them down a mountain ravine.

The parents of both missing women went to the police. They plastered photographs of their daughters all over the region. They even hired private detectives. But weeks turned to months, and there was no sign of Pesce or Luchessa. Meanwhile, Kemper returned to picking up hitchhikers and delivering them safely to their destinations.

Striking Again

On August 15, 1972, hikers found Pesce's skull on Loma Prieta. She was eventually identified by her dental records. But police did not know how she died, and no trace was ever found of Luchessa. The police were unaware that a murderer was in the area and preparing to strike again.

On September 14, Kemper picked up Aiko Koo at a Berkeley bus stop. Aiko was familiar with the route to her dance class in San Francisco. When she realized Kemper was not taking the right road, she grew alarmed. He pulled out his gun and told Aiko that he wanted to kill himself, not her. He was depressed and wanted company. If she came with him and kept quiet, she would be fine.

Kemper drove to an isolated area of the mountains above Santa Cruz and pulled off the road. When he ordered Aiko to get

"It's a bit like playing Russian roulette, except that I'm not the one who risks death. I'm flirting with danger. . . . I know that at any moment I can strike, and it's something that excites me."[8]

—Edmund Kemper, discussing picking up hitchhikers

Police can compare dental record X-rays from potential victims to those of skulls in order to identify human remains.

into the back seat, she complied. Too tall to climb over the seat himself, Kemper got out of the car and slammed the door. Then he realized the back door was locked. His key was in the ignition and his handgun was on the front seat. This was Aiko's chance to escape.

But Kemper stayed calm. He knocked on the rear window and told Aiko to open the door. Perhaps fear had stunned the girl. Perhaps she trusted Kemper when he said he would not hurt her. No one knows why Aiko opened the door for the man, but she did. He climbed into the back seat.

Kemper taped Aiko's mouth and laid on top of her while pinching her nostrils shut. The girl lost consciousness. Kemper raped, strangled, and killed her.

Kemper put Aiko's body in the trunk and headed toward home. On the way, he stopped at a bar for a couple of beers. The next morning at his apartment, Kemper dismembered the girl. Then he disposed of Aiko's body parts in wooded areas off several mountain roads. He kept her head and hands to prevent police from identifying her if the rest of her body was discovered.

Two days later, Kemper had an appointment with two psychiatrists in Fresno. He worried that his nosy landlord might enter his apartment while he was gone and find Aiko's head. So he took the remains with him. After the appointment, Kemper dug a shallow grave in a ravine above Boulder Creek in the Santa Cruz Mountains. There he buried Aiko's head and hands.

CANNIBALISM

Kemper engaged in cannibalism, eating human flesh, after murdering Aiko Koo. When asked why, Kemper said, "Having hunted animals in Montana, I was just pursuing an experiment in cannibalism."[9] Kemper said that he felt a sense of ownership over Aiko afterward.

Aiko's remains were found near Boulder Creek after Kemper was caught.

CHAPTER 6

SERIAL KILLER ON THE LOOSE

n January 1973, Kemper returned the handgun he had borrowed from a friend and bought a .22 caliber automatic pistol. "I went bananas after I got that .22," Kemper said. "This fantastic passion. . . . It was overwhelming me."[1] On January 8, 1973, he sought his next victim.

Conditions were perfect for Kemper's plans as he cruised the streets of Santa Cruz. A hard rain fell. Hitchhikers were desperate for a ride. Kemper gave two college women a ride, but he decided not to kill them. Too many people had seen them get into his car. Just as Kemper was becoming impatient,

Hitchhikers often hold out a thumb to indicate they need a ride.

LESSONS
ROCK N ROLL
AHA
LOST OUR LEASE
MUST VACATE THESE PREMISES
MOVING SALE
EVERY ITEM MUST BE SOLD TO THE BARE WALLS
SAVINGS UP TO 60%

he spotted a lone young woman on Mission Avenue with her thumb out.

Co-Ed Number Four

Eighteen-year-old Cynthia Schall was a student at Cabrillo College, which was near her house. Normally she walked to class. But that day it was raining.

Kemper picked up Schall, showed her his new gun, and drove up into the hills. Toying with the young woman, he told Schall he was suicidal. He just wanted company and would not hurt her. Kemper tucked the gun under his leg to calm Schall down.

Before he killed himself, Kemper told her, he wanted to stop by his mother's house to say goodbye. He parked and ordered Schall to climb into the trunk. She was suspicious and hesitated, but Kemper was persuasive. He was not going to hurt her. He even made a pillow for her head out of a blanket. Then, just as Schall was climbing into the trunk, Kemper shot her in the head.

Kemper drove to his mother's house with

–Edmund Kemper, explaining his thoughts about how quickly Cynthia Schall died

Schall's corpse in the trunk. He barely had time to hide the body in the closet before Clarnell came home from work. After his mother left the next morning, Kemper performed his post-murder ritual of dismemberment and necrophilia.

Later that day, Kemper disposed of Schall's body parts off State Route 1, in an area known as Big Sur. The highway winds for miles on a cliff alongside the ocean. This beautiful stretch of country is often busy. The fact that Kemper had picked up a hitchhiker so close to home and disposed of her body in a popular area was out of the norm for him.

Kemper decided to keep Schall's head close. He buried her head next to a stepping stone in the courtyard of his mother's duplex, positioning it so the eye sockets faced his bedroom window. "Sometimes at night, I talked to her," Kemper said. "Saying love things, the way you do to a girlfriend or a wife."[3]

HEADLESS

Kemper's obsession with beheading began early in life. At age eight, he was fascinated by a magic show with a mock guillotine. Kemper pulled the heads off his sisters' Barbie dolls and severed the heads of cats he killed. He beheaded almost all his victims. Kemper explained that the women's heads "were a bit like a trophy. You know, the head is where everything is at, the brain, eyes, mouth. That's the person."[4]

Motorcyclists sometimes speed over the cliffs along Route 1. An officer was doing a routine check of the area, looking for any accidents, when he found Schall's body.

A Grisly Discovery

When Schall did not return home from class on January 9, her roommate called Schall's parents. They reported her missing to the police immediately. This time the police did not dismiss Schall as a runaway, because evidence of something sinister turned up.

On January 10, 1973, a highway patrol officer stopped on Route 1 where it ran along a tall cliff. The officer spotted what looked like an arm sticking out of a bag. When he investigated, he discovered two arms, strips of skin, and parts of two legs. In the following days, a woman's severed pelvis washed up in a cove south of Santa Cruz. A surfer also found a left hand.

On January 24, pathologists identified the dismembered corpse as the missing co-ed Cynthia Schall. But Schall's disappearance was not the only case for the authorities to investigate. Soon they had two more dismembered bodies on their hands.

Escalation

On February 5, Kemper and his mother had what Kemper called "a real tiff."[5] Blood boiling, he said he was going to a movie. Instead, he looked for another victim.

Rain fell hard as Kemper entered the University of California, Santa Cruz, campus at about 8:30 that evening. Rosalind Thorpe, age 22, was a student there who lived off campus. She had been studying at the library and was waiting at the bus stop when Kemper spotted her.

He pulled over and rolled down the window. "The bus is gone," Kemper told Thorpe. "I've missed it before too. Can I give you a lift? It's pretty late."[6] He noticed Thorpe glance at the campus parking sticker on his car. Kemper's mother had given it to him. Thorpe seemed to take it as evidence that Kemper was a student like her, and she climbed into the car.

Thorpe was chatty and at ease. In moments, Kemper decided, "I was gonna get her, definitely."[7] Then he noticed a hitchhiker and pulled over.

Alice Liu must have seen Thorpe sitting in the front seat beside Kemper. She may have felt comfortable accepting a ride from a couple. Liu got in the back seat, and Kemper took off. Minutes later, they were on a deserted stretch of road, the lights of Santa Cruz glowing below. Kemper slowed down. He told the women this was to better see the view.

While Thorpe was looking out the passenger window, Kemper pulled out his handgun and shot her in the back of the head. Without even stopping the car, Kemper turned around and fired at Liu. She darted around in the back seat, covering her face with her hands. Kemper shot at her twice and missed. The third shot hit her in the temple.

Kemper could hear Liu dying in the back seat. Once outside the city, he pulled over and shot her again. He stuffed both women in the trunk.

Kemper returned to his mother's house and parked on the street. It was 10:30 at night. Anyone could walk by and see him. Kemper disregarded caution and decapitated both women in the back of his car.

FORENSIC SPOTLIGHT

corpse Identification

Police use various tools to identify victims if their bodies are found. Kemper concealed the identity of his victims by decapitating them and sometimes cutting off their hands. At that time, authorities identified corpses through fingerprint analysis, dental records, and X-rays.

Fingerprints show the ridges and furrows on the pads of fingers and thumbs. People leave prints on all kinds of surfaces. No two people, not even identical twins, have the same fingerprints. When a hand washed up on shore a few days after Cynthia Schall disappeared, its fingerprints matched those police found and recorded in her apartment. Police realized then that she was not a runaway but a murder victim.

Dental records also help police identify remains. This method is called forensic odontology. Teeth remain intact long after muscle and tissue have rotted away. Pathologists can match a corpse's teeth with the dental records of a missing person.

Police used both dental records and X-rays to confirm the identity of Schall's body. X-rays are medical images that create pictures of a person's bones and tissue. An X-ray of Schall's corpse matched X-rays she had received when she fractured her arm earlier in life.

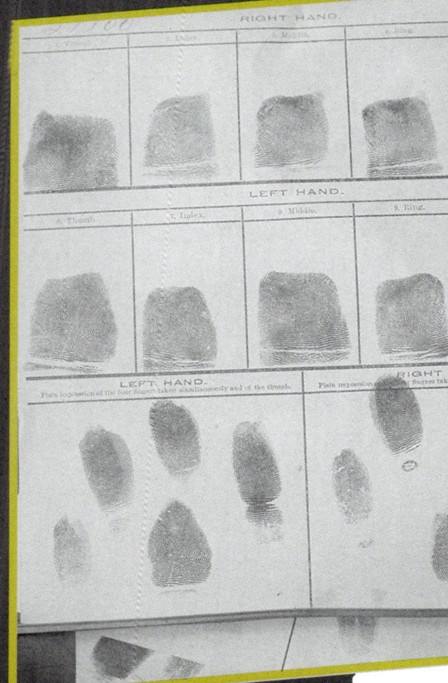

In order to identify a body using fingerprint analysis, investigators must have access to a suspected victim's fingerprints from before the individual disappeared.

Kemper later said that any time he showed hitchhikers his gun, he knew he would have to kill them. Otherwise his potential victims would go to the police.

The next morning, he brought their heads inside and cleaned them. Kemper again committed necrophilia. This time, he did not dismember the women. He had grown bored with the practice. After dark, Kemper drove north and rolled both women's bodies over the edge of Eden Canyon Road. Then he threw their heads over the cliff at an area called Devil's Slide.

On Alert

On February 8, newspapers announced the disappearance of Thorpe and Liu, sparking alarm in Santa Cruz. Search parties combed the Santa Cruz campus. Three days later, the body of Mary Guilfoyle, a co-ed who went missing the previous year, was discovered. Although Kemper was not Guilfoyle's killer, fear rose in the public.

In mid-February, a county road crew discovered two headless corpses lying in a steep ravine. A hiker on Devil's Slide discovered a decaying human skull, and a police search turned up a second skull nearby. On February 23, these remains were identified as those of Thorpe and Liu.

Newspapers assigned the unknown murderer a variety of names—the Chopper, the Butcher, and the Co-Ed Killer. The last nickname stuck. Police spoke on campuses, warning female students not to hitchhike. Universities started shuttle services to discourage hitchhiking. Gun sales spiked. News accounts were often exaggerated, describing victims being found drained of blood or women's bodies being dismembered while they were still alive.

Still some girls continued to hitchhike, and Kemper continued to pick them up. A few students even talked to him about the murdered women. "The second they started talking about that," Kemper said, "they were getting a free ride. . . . They judged me not to be that guy."[10] Therefore, Kemper spared their lives.

But Kemper was getting sloppy. He later said, "As my crimes went on, I became more and more ill, and I took fewer and fewer precautions."[11] Despite this carelessness, police did not have Kemper on their radar as a suspect.

On February 23, Santa Cruz law enforcement admitted to the media that they "had no clues" who the murderer was.[12] Kemper continued to boldly hang out at the Jury Room, rubbing elbows with police and prosecutors. Outwardly he was the same friendly man he had been for months. Inside he was deteriorating.

Kemper said that he was almost always under the influence of drugs or alcohol, except when he was committing crimes.

THE FINAL ACT

By April 1973, the panic in Santa Cruz had calmed down. No more co-eds had disappeared. Things seemed to go back to normal. But Kemper felt anything but normal. Low on money, he moved back into his mother's house. His desire to kill swelled, but he was tired of his old routine.

Kemper fantasized about doing something bigger and bolder. "Toward the end, I became sicker, bloodthirsty, and yet these streams of blood annoyed me. . . . What I long for is to witness death, and to savor the triumph . . . my own triumph over the death of others."[1]

Kemper and his sister spoke about the co-ed killings in April 1973. She said their conversations were brief, and she had no idea he was involved.

Kemper owned many guns. He worried that the police would find his .22 pistol, which was a murder weapon, when they arrived at his house.

Police Contact

In early April, Kemper bought another handgun. When a county records clerk did a routine check on recent gun purchases, she found the form for Kemper's gun registration. The information on the form was blacked out because his juvenile record was sealed. However, through the black ink, the clerk could read "187 PC Madera, California." In California, 187 is the penal code for murder.

Kemper was a convicted felon and had served time in a mental institution. Therefore, he could not legally own a gun. However, because his juvenile record was sealed, he was in a gray area under the law. Still, the sheriff ordered police to go to Kemper's house and confiscate the gun.

On April 6, Kemper arrived at his mother's house to find two police officers there. Sergeant Michael Aluffi told Kemper he needed to confiscate the man's .44 Magnum. Convinced the police knew about the murders, Kemper was prepared to open the trunk, grab his handgun, and kill both detectives. However, Aluffi took Kemper's keys and opened the trunk himself. Although Kemper had killed and dismembered multiple women in the trunk over the last year, the officer did not notice anything abnormal. He gave Kemper a receipt for the gun and left.

The incident rattled Kemper. To make matters worse, tension was high between him and his mother. Kemper said their fights triggered his desire to kill. But he wanted to stop killing students. "It's got to stay between me and my mother," he thought.[2]

Kemper decided to test his ability to resist the temptation to kill. A few days before Easter, he drove to Berkeley and picked up two college students in almost the same spot where he had picked up his first victims, Pesce and Luchessa. These women even physically resembled the women he had killed.

The students wanted a ride back to their dorm. Kemper knew how to get there, but the women wanted him to take a route that happened to lead to the spot where he had murdered Pesce and Luchessa. Kemper's mind reeled. "I'm saying to myself, 'Oh my God. All I [have to] do is relax and they'll take me to their deaths.'"[3]

Kemper resisted temptation and dropped the women off at their dorm unharmed. But he thought that if his mother did not die, more college women would. That was the moment Kemper decided to kill his mother.

–Edmund Kemper, explaining why he murdered co-eds

Final Act

On April 20, 1973, Kemper went to his mother's house with an Easter lily as a gift for her. Clarnell was not home. Kemper drank a six-pack of beer while he waited for her return. Kemper napped as the hours passed.

Clarnell finally came home very late. At about 4:00 a.m. Kemper awoke and found his mother in bed, just turning off her light. She sighed when she saw him. "I suppose you want to sit up all night and talk now," Kemper recalls her saying.[4]

Kemper did want to talk. He had hoped the last conversation he had with his mother would be positive, and her apparent irritation stung. Clarnell said they could talk in the morning, so he said goodnight and left the bedroom.

For an hour, Kemper sat on his bed, working up the nerve to carry out the gruesome task he had set for himself. At 5:00 a.m. he retrieved a hammer from the kitchen and opened his pocketknife. Then he tiptoed into his mother's bedroom. She was asleep on her side. Kemper stared at her for a long moment, then raised the hammer and brought it down hard on his mother's right temple.

Kemper dropped the hammer and stepped back, watching for his mother's reaction. There was none. Blood ran down her face, and her breathing was labored. Kemper rolled his mother over, pulled her head back, and slashed her throat.

Kemper then decapitated her, carried his mother's head

–Edmund Kemper, discussing the murder of his mother

into the living room, and put it on a shelf. For an hour, he screamed at it. Then he threw darts at his mother's head. As a final humiliation to his mother, Kemper returned to the bedroom and performed sexual acts on her corpse.

Kemper dragged the corpse into the closet. He left the house and cruised around until he met a male friend, with whom he drank a few beers. When Kemper returned home, it dawned on him that his mother would be missed.

The next day was Easter. Kemper's mother was supposed to be his final victim, but when the police found Clarnell's body, he would be the primary suspect. So he decided one more person must die to throw the police off his trail. The victim would be his mother's friend, Sally Hallett.

Kemper called Hallett and invited her to go out to dinner with him and his mother that evening. She arrived at Clarnell's house at about 7:30 p.m. Kemper opened the door, telling Hallett that his mother was still getting ready. As the woman walked to the living room, Kemper crooked his arm around her neck, squeezed, and lifted her off the ground. Hallett's neck snapped.

To make absolutely sure Hallett was dead, Kemper taped her mouth shut and tied a bag around her head. He stripped her, laid her on his bed, and emptied her wallet. Then Kemper went to sleep in his mother's blood-soaked bed.

On the Run

When Kemper awoke the next morning, he knew that he was in danger of discovery. Even with Hallett's murder as a distraction, the police would surely still tag Kemper as a primary suspect when they discovered the dead women. He decided to run.

He loaded Hallett's vehicle with his knives, guns, and ammunition, then headed east. When Kemper reached Reno, Nevada, he left Hallett's car at a gas station and rented another vehicle. Then he drove for 18 hours straight, stopping only for gas.

On the drive, Kemper listened to the radio, expecting
to hear that law enforcement had put out an all-points
bulletin on him. This signal would alert all nearby officers
to look out for a suspect. Kemper planned to go out in
a blaze. He vowed to "get my
weapons and go to high ground
and attack the authorities when
they came."[9]

Finally, after driving without
sleep for almost 1,500 miles
(2,400 km), Kemper stopped
in Pueblo, Colorado.[10] There
had been nothing on the radio
about the murder of his mother
and Hallett. When Kemper
realized the police were not

looking for him, he felt exhausted. He wanted the murder
spree to end. So he went to a phone booth and dialed the
Santa Cruz police department.

"I killed my mother and her friend," Kemper told
the officer on the other end of the line. "And I killed
those college girls."[11] Kemper confessed that he was the
Co-Ed Killer.

When Kemper called the police, he said he had three guns and 200 rounds of ammunition in his car. He wanted an officer to arrest him so he couldn't go near the weapons.

CONFESSION AND CAPTURE

On April 23, 1973, at about 11:00 p.m., the telephone rang at the Santa Cruz police station. Officer Andrew Crain picked up. The man on the other end of the line wanted to speak to Lieutenant Charles Scherer because, the caller said, "He's been looking for me."[1]

Lieutenant Scherer was not on duty, and Crain refused to call him at home. "This is no prank," the caller said."[2] Call back, Crain instructed. The man did so an hour later. A different officer answered and told the caller to try again in the morning.

The man called again at 5:00 a.m. Officer Jim Conner answered this time. Lieutenant Scherer was still not on duty. When Conner asked the caller what he wanted to talk to Lieutenant Scherer about, the caller screamed, "Co-ed killing!"[3]

Nervous, confused, and rambling, the caller said he was Ed Kemper. He was in Pueblo, Colorado, and about to

Both Clarnell and Hallett worked at the University of California, Santa Cruz. The university held a memorial for the women after they were killed.

have a nervous breakdown. Kemper told Officer Conner what he was calling about: "There was eight people involved. . . . There's eight dead people."[4] Now he had the attention of the police.

Conner asked Kemper for the location of the phone booth he was calling from, and another officer alerted the Pueblo Police Department. To keep Kemper on the line, Conner asked him about the crimes. While Kemper began to talk, Conner could not believe it. He knew Ed Kemper from the Jury Room. He thought of the young man as

NO ONE LEFT

During Kemper's time in jail, officials handed him a booking sheet to fill out. This form contains personal information and a photograph. One question Kemper needed to fill out was who should be notified in case of an emergency. When he got to this question, Kemper paused. Then he quietly asked Sergeant Aluffi if he could put Aluffi's name down as an emergency contact. "I don't have anybody left," Kemper explained.[6] The man had alienated or murdered any family who once cared for him.

"a gentle giant . . . a likable kind of guy."[5]

Perhaps Kemper sensed Conner's suspicion that this call was a prank. He mentioned Sergeant Michael Aluffi, the officer who had confiscated Kemper's gun recently. Kemper pleaded with him to go back to his mother's house. If the police looked in Clarnell's closet, they would know this call was no prank.

Meanwhile, Pueblo patrolman David Martinez responded to the arrest order he heard over the radio. When Martinez reached the address, he saw Kemper inside a phone booth, his back turned and the phone to his ear. Martinez drew his revolver, quietly approached the booth, and tapped on it. Kemper did not put up a fight. He stepped out of the phone booth and allowed Martinez to search and cuff him.

Backup arrived a couple of minutes later. Local officers secured Kemper and searched his car. They found a shotgun, a rifle with a sniper scope, an automatic rifle,

Detectives eventually uncovered human remains just beside Kemper's home and in a ravine farther from the house.

knives, sabers, and hundreds of rounds of ammunition in the trunk. Police also found Kemper's bloodstained buckskin jacket.

Sergeant Aluffi went to Clarnell's house as Kemper had requested. Inside he found a nightmare. As Aluffi entered, the stench slapped him in the face. Blood was splattered on the walls and pooled on the floors. Hair lay in clumps everywhere. Blood and body fluids had soaked through to the box spring of Clarnell's bed. Two headless corpses lay piled inside a closet, and police found the two women's heads in another room. In the middle of this horror sat an Easter lily still in bloom.

Buried Bodies

While Kemper began to spill the details of his crimes to the Pueblo police force, Santa Cruz law enforcement authorities caught a plane to Colorado. Accompanying Aluffi were Lieutenant Scherer, Richard Verbrugge from the district attorney's office, and the district attorney himself, Peter Chang.

Kemper was led out of his Pueblo jail cell in handcuffs when the authorities from Santa Cruz arrived. Looking pale and strained, Kemper seemed relieved to see them. Everyone sat down in a conference room, and Lieutenant Scherer turned on a tape recorder. He explained that they were going to talk about the statements Kemper had made to the Pueblo officers. "Are you fully aware of your constitutional rights, Ed?"[8]

At that moment, Kemper cared more about confessing than future legal consequences. He waived his right to have a lawyer present and his right to have an extradition hearing in Colorado. Kemper wanted to go home to California for his trial, so a hearing was not necessary to give law enforcement the right to remove Kemper from Colorado for prosecution.

Terry Medina, *left*, and Paul Daugherty, *right*, were two of the law enforcement officers who searched Kemper's car. They found a shovel in the vehicle.

As the tape recorder whirred, Scherer said, "Tell us whatever details you choose. Do this as though you were writing a letter to a friend in some distant place."[10] And so, the Co-Ed Killer began to tell the tale of the last hours of life for eight women.

In addition to the grisly details of the murders he committed, Kemper also described his rules of operation. The first rule was to observe. If he intended to commit murder on a given day, Kemper would watch the traffic flow and police presence and assess the mood of hitchhikers.

Another rule of operation was that Kemper did not pick up anyone unless they were a target for murder. In his months of practice runs, Kemper sometimes picked up male hitchhikers or a mother and child. But once he became a killer, he only gave rides to co-eds he considered candidates for "possible execution." Kemper's targets included young, good-looking, middle- or upper-class women. He had no interest in hitchhikers who he called "scroungy, messy, dirty, smelly, [hippie] types."[11]

Over the course of four days, the team from Santa Cruz drove Kemper back to California. With Kemper shackled and cuffed in the back seat, they dropped off the rental car in Reno and picked up Sally Hallett's car where Kemper had left it. At night, he stayed in local jails while the Santa Cruz team stayed at motels.

Meanwhile, back in Santa Cruz, law enforcement officers armed with search warrants impounded Kemper's car. Inside was evidence of his crimes. Officers found human hair, a bloodstained back seat, ammunition clips, and a spent bullet lodged in a door panel.

Once back in California, the law enforcement team did not take Kemper directly to jail. First, they drove to San Francisco and around Alameda County where Kemper had rented an apartment for some time. Kemper showed the police where he had picked up his Berkeley victims and where he had buried their remains.

When the group returned to Santa Cruz, a team of 20 officers waited. Word that the Co-Ed Killer was under arrest had leaked, and the press was out in full force. Kemper became upset at the sight of all the cameras. "This is no circus to me, man! Get me out of here."[12]

Once Kemper calmed down, he spent six hours showing detectives around where he killed his victims. In a 20-mile (32 km) radius around his mother's house, police unearthed a pelvis, arm, rib cage, and torso.[13] These remains were later identified as belonging to Mary Anne Pesce, Anita Luchessa, and Aiko Koo. Some of Cynthia Schall's possessions were also discovered.

Next Kemper showed the police officers a spot in Clarnell Kemper's backyard. There they dug up Schall's buried skull. It had remained in its spot below Kemper's bedroom window.

On April 30, 1973, police officers escorted Kemper into a Santa Cruz courtroom. District Attorney Chang charged him with eight counts of first-degree murder.[15] Kemper waived his right to have the charges read. He did not need this formality. The murders were etched in Kemper's memory. The judge denied bail and ordered Kemper to remain in custody until trial.

CHAPTER 9

ON TRIAL AND IN PRISON

O n May 18, 1973, deputies escorted a cuffed and shackled Edmund Kemper into Superior Court in Santa Cruz. Superior Court Judge Harry Brauer informed Kemper that a grand jury had indicted him with eight counts of first-degree murder.[1] Kemper kept his eyes fixed to the floor while he heard the grand jury's decision.

When the judge asked how Kemper pleaded, Kemper said not guilty by reason of insanity. This defense had worked after he murdered his grandparents. Perhaps it would work again.

Kemper's arraignment was on April 30, 1973. At this hearing, he was charged with eight counts of murder.

Peter Chang, *right*, and Richard Verbrugge, *left*, worked together during Kemper's arrest and trial.

Kemper's Trial

Kemper's trial began on October 23, 1973. District Attorney Peter Chang began his opening statement with an apology. He was sorry for the gruesome details the jury was about to hear. Chang said he would prove Kemper was "a sexual deviant and psychopath with no conscience."[2]

The prosecution's case developed in three phases. First, Chang had to prove that a crime had actually been committed. To demonstrate this, parents spoke about their daughters disappearing. College friends described the last time they had seen their roommates.

Officers described the body parts they found scattered across the county and beyond. Pathologists explained the stories told by the dead women's wounds. The mood in the courtroom was grim.

The second phase of the state's case was to prove that it was Kemper who had murdered the eight women. Here Chang used Kemper's own words against him. For hours, the courtroom listened to the graphic descriptions of murder on the tape-recorded confessions. On one tape Kemper said, "I feel personally I was quite insane when I was committing these crimes."[3]

The issue of Kemper's sanity made up the final phase of the prosecution's case. On October 29, three court-appointed psychiatrists took the stand. All of them declared that Kemper was sane when he committed murder. Doctor Donald Lowe said Kemper "knew his acts were evil, was able to [plan his crimes], and able to reflect on the gravity and enormity of his acts."[4] Doctor Joel Fort concluded that it was not insanity that pushed Kemper to murder, but sexual desire.

Chang's final piece of evidence was a videotape of Kemper's confession. As the video played on a television screen in the courtroom, the defendant buried his face in his hands. He sometimes covered his ears.

Next, it was defense attorney James Jackson's turn to prove Kemper was insane. Jackson called one psychiatrist to the stand, but his testimony was dismissed by the court because he used a different definition of insanity than the state's. Allyn Kemper took the stand and talked about her brother's troubled youth. But the primary defense witness was Kemper himself.

Kemper took the stand on November 1. He described the violent fantasies he had been having since he was a young boy. He admitted to fantasizing about killing many people, including District Attorney Chang. At times, Kemper was near tears. He said it was hard to speak about these thoughts because he had kept them secret for so long.

When Jackson asked what Kemper thought of when he killed his victims, Kemper replied, "I wanted the girls for myself—as possessions. They were going to be mine.

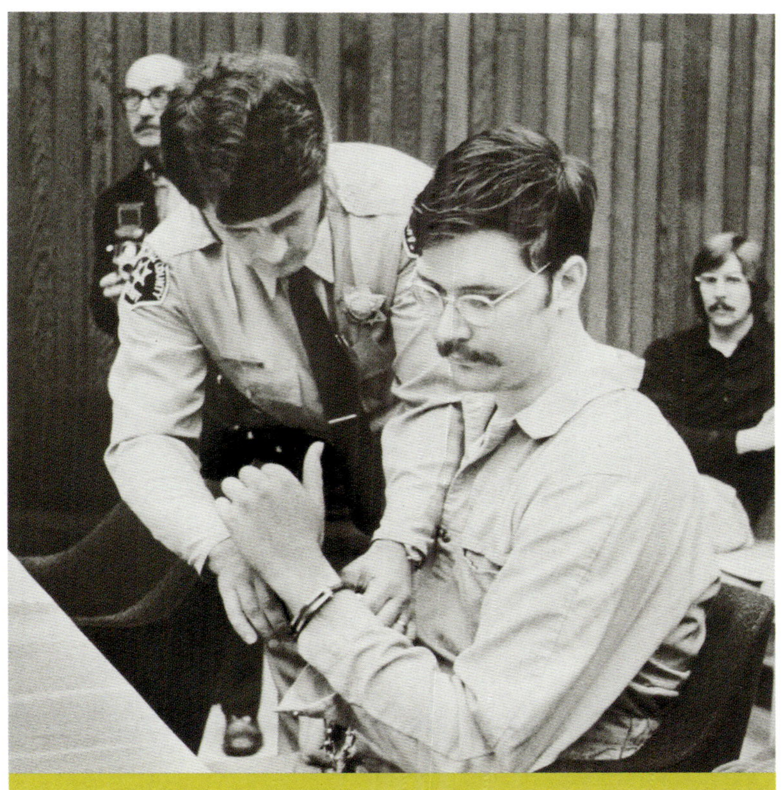

Kemper remained shackled during his trial.

They are mine." Kemper said he turned himself in because he did not want to hurt any more people. "I want help," he said.[5] After this testimony, the defense rested.

Drama was high during closing arguments. Chang called the Kemper case "the most enormous cold-blooded murder case in history." He painted a picture of a cunning man who knew exactly what he was doing. Under the law, Chang said, a defendant's impulse to kill "must be the result of mental disease or defect" in order for him to be found not guilty by reason of insanity.[6] Kemper, Chang said, had no such defect.

Defense Attorney Jackson portrayed Kemper as a tortured soul. "There are two people trapped in the body of a giant," Jackson said. "One acts for good and one acts for evil. They fight each other and have been for years."[7]

On November 8, 1973, the jury deliberated for five hours. The group's verdict was that Kemper was sane and guilty on all counts. The death penalty was not legal in California at the time, so Judge Brauer sentenced Kemper to serve seven years to life for each of his eight victims.[8] The eight sentences were concurrent, meaning they are all served at the same time rather than being served one after another as a much longer prison stay. That also meant Kemper could be eligible for parole after serving seven years behind bars.

However, Kemper could be kept in prison for the rest of his life if his applications for parole were denied. "May God have mercy on your soul," Judge Brauer said to Kemper at his sentencing. "But you understand I have to protect the rest of the people from people like you."[9]

Behind Bars

Kemper was initially sent to the California Medical Facility (CMF) in Vacaville, California, for observation. Some corrections officers called this medium-security facility Disneyland North. They thought the CMF was more comfortable and pleasant than prison. Outside, it looked like any prison, but the inside was more like a hospital.

Kemper wanted to stay at the CMF. However, soon he was transferred to Folsom State Prison, a maximum-security prison near Sacramento, California. This was the darkest period of Kemper's incarceration.

> "I really wasn't surprised when it came out that way. There was just no way they could find me insane. . . . Society just isn't ready for that yet."[10]
>
> *–Edmund Kemper after he was sentenced in 1973*

He struggled to not take his own life. Because his mental health was so fragile, prison officials periodically returned Kemper to the CMF for treatment. Finally, in 1977, he was transferred there permanently.

Model Inmate

Kemper did not want to jeopardize his ability to remain at the CMF, so he worked hard to be a good inmate. He volunteered to be a case study. Doctors who wanted to help mentally ill people probed his brain through therapy. Journalists interviewed him about the details of his crimes. FBI agents seeking to catch the next serial killer tried to figure out what made Kemper tick.

Kemper also participated in the Blind Project, a program operated by the Volunteers of Vacaville. He read books aloud, recording the audio on cassettes for visually impaired people. By 1987, Kemper had read 5,000 hours and supervised 15 other inmates involved in the project. He even received two trophies for his work. When a visually impaired couple who appreciated his work visited Kemper, he was deeply moved. "I can't begin to tell you what this . . . meant to me, to be able to do something constructive for someone else," he said.[11]

Understanding Edmund Kemper

People involved in his case have struggled to make sense of Edmund Kemper. Doctor Donald Lunde, the author of a book examining the role mental health plays in murderers' actions, evaluated Kemper after he was incarcerated. Lunde considered him to be a sociopath who was incurable.

John Douglas was an FBI agent who interviewed Kemper extensively and used the knowledge gained

Inmates at the California Medical Facility are either chronically or terminally ill, including those who suffer from mental illnesses.

from these conversations to help create an investigative tool called criminal profiling. He admitted to liking Kemper, which illustrated the man's danger. According to Douglas, many sociopaths are "quite charming, highly articulate."[12] They use this charm to lure in their victims.

Psychiatrist Joel Fort testified at some of Kemper's parole hearings. He did not want Kemper ever released. To Kemper, Fort said, "killing is as acceptable as eating a meal or brushing your teeth."[13]

Tom Honig was a reporter for the *Santa Cruz Sentinel* who attended every day of Kemper's trial. Honig said, "I think there's a side of him that would have given anything to be a normal person. There's part of Ed Kemper that is as horrified and disgusted with what he did as we are."[14]

Edmund Kemper's case helped the FBI develop criminal profiling. Criminal profiles explain likely characteristics about criminals. This tool helps law enforcement catch offenders by narrowing down the field of suspects.

In the late 1960s and early 1970s, the number of murders in the United States skyrocketed, and many remained unsolved. But some of the criminals had been caught. FBI agents John Douglas and Robert Ressler interviewed criminals to learn about the motivations behind their attacks.

The first killer the agents interviewed was Kemper. Douglas said Kemper was the perfect case study because he had a great memory and spoke directly. Douglas and Ressler then teamed up with a professor of psychiatric nursing. By 1983, the team had completed a study from interviews with dozens of killers.

Criminal profiles may include a photo of the suspect if officers have one available.

The study revealed common patterns of criminal behavior. FBI agents and detectives use these patterns to filter evidence from crime scenes in order to create a mental and physical profile of possible suspects. For example, police might find clues that show a killer plans their crimes ahead of time and leaves little evidence behind. A psychological profile might speculate that this criminal has an organized life outside their crimes. They are likely employed and may live with a partner. These details can help law enforcement search for suspects.

These responses offer insights into the man, but insights are little consolation to the loved ones of Kemper's victims. Over the decades, Kemper has been denied parole multiple times. At his 2017 hearing, Kemper's cousin testified against him. She wanted to set the record straight about her grandparents, who she said were "both very intelligent, very loving people."[15]

She could not imagine the pain the families of the murdered women felt, but she did know what it meant to lose her grandparents. "How can we take a risk of sending this man out again?" She told the parole board, "I don't care how old he gets."[16] Kemper remained incarcerated in CMF in 2024. He was in his seventies and increasingly frail.

ESSENTIAL FACTS

TIMELINE

Dec. 18, 1948: Edmund Kemper III is born in Burbank, California.

Aug. 27, 1964: Kemper kills his grandparents, Maude and Edmund Kemper I.

Dec. 6, 1964: Kemper is institutionalized in the Atascadero State Hospital for the Criminally Insane.

Dec. 18, 1969: Kemper is released from state custody.

May 7, 1972: Kemper kills college students Mary Ann Pesce and Anita Luchessa.

Sept. 14, 1972: Kemper kills high school student Aiko Koo.

Jan. 8, 1973: Kemper kills college student Cynthia Schall.

Jan. 24, 1973: Police identify the dismembered remains of Cynthia Schall.

Feb. 5, 1973: Kemper kills college students Rosalind Thorpe and Alice Liu. When their bodies are identified soon after, the police realize there is a serial killer on the loose.

Apr. 21, 1973: Kemper kills his mother and her friend Sally Hallett.

Apr. 24, 1973: Kemper is arrested in Pueblo, Colorado, after calling the police to confess his crimes.

Nov. 8, 1973: A jury finds Kemper guilty of eight counts of first-degree murder, and he is sentenced to serve seven years to life for each of the eight victims.

IMPACT ON SOCIETY

Edmund Kemper's murder spree impacted society in important ways. His crimes took the lives of eight people. His legal case also raised questions about when, if ever, a defendant should be found not guilty by reason of insanity. While Kemper was found guilty, his case highlighted the challenge of protecting society from dangerous criminals while balancing the rights of people with mental illnesses they may have difficulty managing.

Kemper's case also helped the FBI develop the tool of criminal profiling. Law enforcement officers used insights gained from their extensive interviews with Kemper, in which he discussed why and how he committed his crimes, to develop a template for analyzing evidence found at crime scenes. Detectives can match this evidence to potential suspects to help catch criminals.

QUOTE

"The only time people got killed was when [Clarnell] and I were fighting like cats and dogs. I couldn't vent it any other way. . . . I think [the co-eds] were surrogates. I was killing her, not them."

—*Edmund Kemper, explaining why he murdered co-eds*

GLOSSARY

decapitate

To cut off the head of a person.

defendant

An individual accused in a court of law.

dismember

To cut a body into separate pieces.

district attorney

A public official who acts as prosecutor for a county.

emasculate

To deprive someone, usually a man, of strength and vigor, where those traits are considered valuable and ideal in men.

grand jury

A jury gathered before a criminal trial to determine if there is enough evidence to try a defendant for a particular crime.

morbidity

A state of mind in which a person has a lot of somber, unwholesome feelings.

parole

The supervised release of a prisoner before the full completion of their sentence, after which the person has to maintain good behavior for a certain period of time.

pathologist

A doctor who studies body fluids and tissues.

premonition

A strong feeling that something unpleasant is about
to happen.

prosecutor

A lawyer who leads the case against a defendant in court.

psychiatrist

A doctor who specializes in diagnosing and treating
mental illness.

sociopath

Someone who may be diagnosed with antisocial
personality disorder or who also shows frequent, severe
antisocial behavior, such as hostility and disregard for
others' feelings.

surrogate

An object or person that stands in for someone or
something else.

titillate

To stimulate or excite someone.

SELECTED BIBLIOGRAPHY

Cheney, Margaret. *The Coed Killer*. Walker & Co., 1976.

Douglas, John, and Mark Olshaker. *Mindhunter: Inside the FBI's Elite Serial Crime Unit*. Simon & Schuster, 1995.

Matera, Dary. *Ed Kemper*. Sterling, 2021.

FURTHER READINGS

Fleming, Candace. *Murder Among Friends: How Leopold and Loeb Tried to Commit the Perfect Crime*. Anne Schwartz, 2022.

Mooney, Carla. *Jeffrey Dahmer*. Abdo, 2024.

Morris, Rebecca. *Joseph James DeAngelo: The Golden State Killer*. Abdo, 2025.

ONLINE RESOURCES

To learn more about serial killers, please visit **abdobooklinks.com** or scan this QR code. These links are routinely monitored and updated to provide the most current information available.

MORE INFORMATION

For more information on this subject, contact or visit the following organizations:

ALCATRAZ EAST CRIME MUSEUM

2757 Pkwy.
Pigeon Forge, TN 37863
alcatrazeast.com

The Alcatraz East Crime Museum takes visitors on a deep dive into US crime history. Five galleries explore criminal profiles, the penal system, victims' stories, crime prevention, forensic science, law enforcement, and the justice system.

THE FBI EXPERIENCE

FBI Headquarters
935 Pennsylvania Ave. NW
Washington, DC 20535

The FBI Experience is a self-guided tour at FBI Headquarters. The tour showcases interactive multimedia displays and artifacts that tell the history of the FBI and how it currently functions as a law enforcement agency.

NATIONAL LAW ENFORCEMENT MUSEUM

444 E St. NW
Washington, DC 20001
nleomf.org/museum/

The National Law Enforcement Museum contains more than 25,000 artifacts from more than 300 years of US law enforcement history. The museum educates the public about the role of law enforcement officers.

SOURCE NOTES

CHAPTER 1. GONE MISSING

1. Dary Matera. *Ed Kemper*. Sterling, 2021. 68.
2. Matera, *Ed Kemper*, 24.
3. Matera, *Ed Kemper*, 70.

CHAPTER 2. A TROUBLED CHILDHOOD

1. Dary Matera. *Ed Kemper*. Sterling, 2021. 1.
2. Margaret Cheney. *The Coed Killer*. Walker & Co., 1976. 8.
3. Matera, *Ed Kemper*, 3.
4. Matera, *Ed Kemper*, 6.
5. Matera, *Ed Kemper*, 7.
6. Matera, *Ed Kemper*, 11.
7. Matera, *Ed Kemper*, 12.
8. Matera, *Ed Kemper*, 12.
9. Matera, *Ed Kemper*, 10.
10. Matera, *Ed Kemper*, 13.

CHAPTER 3. MURDER AND ATASCADERO

1. Marj von Beroldingen. "Edmund Kemper Interview." *Front Page Detective*, Mar. 1974, truecrime.net. Accessed 22 Mar. 2024.
2. Dary Matera. *Ed Kemper*. Sterling, 2021. 17.
3. Beroldingen, "Edmund Kemper Interview."
4. "'I Just Wanted to See What It Felt Like to Shoot Grandma.'" *Edmund Kemper Stories*, 28 Aug. 2021, edmundkemperstories.com. Accessed 27 Mar. 2024.
5. Matera, *Ed Kemper*, 21.
6. Margaret Cheney. *The Coed Killer*. Walker & Co., 1976. 22.
7. Matera, *Ed Kemper*, 22.
8. "Diagnosis in 1964." *Edmund Kemper Stories*, 28 Dec. 2021, edmundkemperstories.com. Accessed 25 Mar. 2024.
9. Matera, *Ed Kemper*, 24.
10. "'I Was Born There, You Know.'" *Edmund Kemper Stories*, 13 Jan. 2022, edmundkemperstories.com. Accessed 25 Mar. 2024.
11. Matera, *Ed Kemper*, 25.
12. Cheney, *The Coed Killer*, 30.
13. Cheney, *The Coed Killer*, 30.
14. Cheney, *The Coed Killer*, 29.
15. "'They Can't See the Things Going On in My Mind.'" *Edmund Kemper Stories*, 24 Sept. 2020, edmundkemperstories.com. Accessed 20 Mar. 2024.

16. "'Things Going On in My Mind.'"

17. Pat Bauer. "Tate Murders." *Britannica*, n.d., britannica.com. Accessed 4 June 2024.

CHAPTER 4. BACK ON THE STREETS

1. Dary Matera. *Ed Kemper*. Sterling, 2021. 34.

2. Robert K. Ressler and Tom Shachtman. *Whoever Fights Monsters: My Twenty Years Tracking Serial Killers for the FBI*. St. Martin's Press, 1992. 221.

3. Margaret Cheney. *The Coed Killer*. Walker & Co., 1976. 38.

4. Matera, *Ed Kemper*, 40.

5. Matera, *Ed Kemper*, 40.

6. Matera. *Ed Kemper*, 38.

7. Matera. *Ed Kemper*, 41.

8. Matera, *Ed Kemper*, 2.

9. Matera, *Ed Kemper*, 44.

10. Matera, *Ed Kemper*, 45.

11. Cheney, *The Coed Killer*, 42.

12. Matera, *Ed Kemper*, 42.

CHAPTER 5. THE CO-ED KILLER STRIKES

1. Margaret Cheney. *The Coed Killer*. Walker & Co., 1976. 86.

2. Cheney, *The Coed Killer*, 87.

3. Dary Matera. *Ed Kemper*. Sterling, 2021. 48.

4. "'This Girl Was Actually Fighting Me, Almost Succeeding.'" *Edmund Kemper Stories*, 22 Sept. 2019, edmundkemperstories.com. Accessed 29 Mar. 2024.

5. "'This Girl Was Actually Fighting.'"

6. Matera, *Ed Kemper*, 55.

7. Cheney, *The Coed Killer*, 50.

8. Matera, *Ed Kemper*, 59.

9. Matera, *Ed Kemper*, 71.

CHAPTER 6. SERIAL KILLER ON THE LOOSE

1. Dary Matera. *Ed Kemper*. Sterling, 2021. 77.

2. Matera, *Ed Kemper*, 80.

3. Matera, *Ed Kemper*, 80.

4. "'Of Course, the Personality Is Gone.'" *Edmund Kemper Stories*, 18 Mar. 2020, edmundkemperstories.com. Accessed 31 Mar. 2024.

5. Margaret Cheney. *The Coed Killer*. Walker & Co., 1976. 117.

6. Cheney, *The Coed Killer*, 87.

7. Cheney, *The Coed Killer*, 120.

8. Matera, *Ed Kemper*, 86.

9. "Kemper's Victims' Manner of Death." *Edmund Kemper Stories*, 24 Oct. 2023, edmundkemperstories.com. Accessed 31 Mar. 2024.

10. Matera, *Ed Kemper*, 85.

11. Matera, *Ed Kemper*, 94.

12. Matera, *Ed Kemper*, 110.

13. Crystal Bonvillian. "Serial Killer Who Said He Killed to Ward Off Earthquakes Dies at 75." *KIRO7*, 23 Aug. 2022, kiro7.com. Accessed 31 Mar. 2024.

14. Matera, *Ed Kemper*, 98.

CHAPTER 7. THE FINAL ACT

1. Dary Matera. *Ed Kemper*. Sterling, 2021. 105.

2. "Edmund Kemper Interview in 1984." *YouTube*. Uploaded by True Crime Magazine, 12 June 2016, youtube.com. Accessed 1 Apr. 2024.

3. "Edmund Kemper Interview in 1984."

4. Matera, *Ed Kemper*, 113.

5. Matera, *Ed Kemper*, 109.

6. "'I Missed All This by Forty Hours.'" *Edmund Kemper Stories*, 12 Feb. 2023, edmundkemperstories.com. Accessed 1 Apr. 2024.

7. "The Murder of Clarnell Strandberg." *Edmund Kemper Stories*, 21 Apr. 2021, edmundkemperstories.com. Accessed 1 Apr. 2024.

8. "Ed Kemper's Last Victim—Sally Hallett." *Edmund Kemper Stories*, 17 July 2021, edmundkemperstories.com. Accessed 1 Apr. 2024.

9. Matera, *Ed Kemper*, 123.

10. Matera, *Ed Kemper*, 122.

11. Matera, *Ed Kemper*, 122.

12. "Edmund Kemper's Cryptic Note." *Edmund Kemper Stories*, 6 Mar. 2019, edmundkemperstories.com. Accessed 1 Apr. 2024.

CHAPTER 8. CONFESSION AND CAPTURE

1. Margaret Cheney. *The Coed Killer*. Walker & Co., 1976. 72.

2. Cheney, *The Coed Killer*, 73.

3. Cheney, *The Coed Killer*, 74.

4. Cheney, *The Coed Killer*, 75.

5. Dary Matera. *Ed Kemper*. Sterling, 2021. 126.

6. Matera, *Ed Kemper*, 139.

7. Matera, *Ed Kemper*, 124.

8. Cheney, *The Coed Killer*, 83.

9. Cathy Redfern. "Chang's Big Murder Cases." *Santa Cruz Sentinel*, 14 Dec. 2004, A-8, history.santacruzpl.org. Accessed 4 June 2024.

10. Cheney, *The Coed Killer*, 84.

11. Cheney, *The Coed Killer*, 143.

12. Matera, *Ed Kemper*, 136.

13. Matera, *Ed Kemper*, 136.

14. Lari Blumenfeld. "Aiko Just Vanished: Our Lost People." *San Diego Independent*, 3 Jan. 1973, newspapers.com. Accessed 8 Apr. 2024.

15. Matera, *Ed Kemper*, 146.

CHAPTER 9. ON TRIAL AND IN PRISON

1. Dary Matera. *Ed Kemper*. Sterling, 2021. 146.

2. "D.A. Details Decapitation of Eight Woman." *San Diego Independent*, 24 Oct. 1973, 2, newspapers.com. Accessed 3 Apr. 2024.

3. "Thrill of Killing Described." *Progress Bulletin*, 26 Oct. 1973, 2, newspapers.com. Accessed 4 Apr. 2024.

4. "Psychiatrist Finds Kemper Sane." *San Diego Independent*, 30 Oct. 1973, 29, newspapers.com. Accessed 4 Apr. 2024.

5. Margaret Cheney. *The Coed Killer*. Walker & Co., 1976. 171.

6. Tom Honig. "Final Arguments Presented Today in Kemper Trial." *Santa Cruz Sentinel*, 7 Nov. 1973, newspapers.com. Accessed 4 Apr. 2024.

7. Honig, "Final Arguments Presented."

8. Matera, *Ed Kemper*, 166.

9. Dary Matera. *Ed Kemper*. Sterling, 2021. 166.

10. Marj von Beroldingen. "Edmund Kemper Interview." *Front Page Detective*, Mar. 1974, truecrime.net. Accessed 22 Mar. 2024.

11. Matera, *Ed Kemper*, 177–178

12. "'I Would Be Less Than Honest If I Didn't Admit That I Liked Ed.'" *Edmund Kemper Stories*, 26 Aug. 2019, edmundkemperstories.com. Accessed 4 June 2024.

13. Matera, *Ed Kemper*, 218.

14. Matera, *Ed Kemper*, 219.

15. "Subsequent Parole Consideration Hearing, State of California Board of Parole Hearings." *Edmund Kemper Stories*, 25 July 2017, 143–144, edmundkemperstories.com. Accessed 5 Apr. 2024.

16. "Subsequent Parole Consideration Hearing," 143–144.

17. Matt Grobar. "'Mindhunter' Breakout Cameron Britton Taps into Psychology & Cold Intelligence of Real-Life Serial Killer Edmund Kemper." *Deadline*, 14 June 2018, deadline.com. Accessed 1 July 2024.

INDEX

JUDY DODGE CUMMINGS

Judy Dodge Cummings is the author of more than 25 books for children and teenagers on topics ranging from history to hip-hop. She writes from her home in southern Wisconsin.